Brainstorming

A Creative Guide to Help Parents and Children
Through Severe Weather

By Katie Horner

Illustrations by Neil Nakahodo

KANSAS CITY STAR BOOKS

Brainstorming
A Creative Guide to Help Parents
and Children Through Severe Weather

By Katie Horner

Editor: Evie Rapport
Designer: Amy Robertson
Illustrations and information graphics: Neil Nakahodo

 KANSAS CITY STAR BOOKS

Published by Kansas City Star Books
1729 Grand Blvd.
Kansas City, MO 64108

First edition, first printing
ISBN: 978-1-933466-73-6

Printed by Walsworth Publishing Co., Marceline, Mo.

Contents

About the Author

Katie Horner is a mother and the award-winning Chief Meteorologist at KCTV-5 in Kansas City, Mo. Her passion for tornadoes and tornado safety began in 1975, when she was a small child in Bellevue, Neb. That year a monster tornado hit her community. She will never forget what it felt like to huddle in a storm shelter while the destructive winds roared above, how it felt to climb out of the shelter across broken glass, boards and furniture covered with strewn insulation. She has dedicated her life to helping others during the terrifying time when a tornado strikes.

She studied weather at the University of Maryland and finished her degree at Mississippi State University. She also holds degrees in public relations and marketing from the University of West Florida. Katie forecast the weather at WEAR in Pensacola, Fla., from 1989 to 1994. Hurricane Andrew came up the Gulf of Mexico during her watch.

In May 1994, she and her family moved to Kansas City, and she has been at KCTV ever since. A member of the American Meteorological Society, she has earned its Seal of Approval and served on its board from 2004 to 2008.

Katie is married to Frank Armato. She has three daughters, Chelsea, Anna and Ava.

Dedications

To my encouraging husband, Frank, who would not let me give up on this project.

To my daughters, who were unwitting test subjects for the techniques in this book.

To my parents, Tom and Pat, who taught me by example to care passionately about every member of our community.

To psychologist Janice A. Myers, who confirmed that the techniques in this book are based on sound child-behavioral theories and practices.

Brainstorming

A Creative Guide to Help Parents and Children Through Severe Weather

As a meteorologist, I have helped many people through terrifying storms. As a mother, I have held my children when storms rolled overhead. I have taught them to be appreciative and respectful of the awesome power of nature.

I know thunderstorms can be scary. They can fill the sky with flashes of light. When thunder roars, it can shake the whole house. The wind can bend and break trees and damage houses. Hail can dent cars. Sometimes it can rain so hard the water flows out of the creeks and over the roads.

It is normal to be afraid of thunderstorms. Many people are. Fear is healthy if it leads to respect and appropriate behavior, like not playing baseball during a thunderstorm. Fear is not good if it consumes you, makes you too afraid to move. I am going to help *you* help your children change any unhealthy fears to fascination, while always remaining respectful of bad weather.

The first step is to learn weather basics. We'll start with what causes weather, how thunderstorms form and how to stay safe around lightning. Enjoy the experiments sprinkled in. We will address fear and how to help a frightened child. Finally, I will give you very specific tips on what to do before, during and after a tornado to keep your family safe and your children calm. Let's begin.

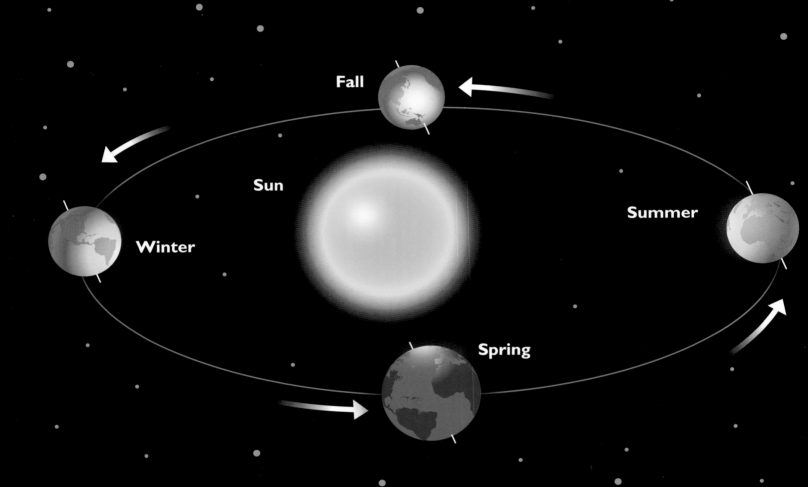

Fall

Sun

Winter

Summer

Spring

The Seasons

In its simplest form, weather is a result of air masses with different temperatures and moisture content moving over the globe. Weather patterns across North America can vary greatly because of these moving air masses.

Mountain ranges, ocean currents and the jet stream can cause some places, like the West Coast, to have few severe thunderstorms. The central Great Plains have the most severe weather because there are no mountain ranges blocking the cold Canadian air from interacting with the warm, moist air that comes off the Gulf of Mexico. So what causes these air masses to move around? It starts with the tilt of the Earth.

The Earth is always tilted 23.5 degrees toward the North Star, or Polaris. (Polaris is the star at the tip of the handle of the Big Dipper constellation.)

The Earth travels in an elliptical loop around the sun each year. Part of the year, the North Pole is pointing toward the sun. This is summer for the Northern Hemisphere (the half of the Earth north of the equator) and winter for the Southern Hemisphere.

Summer is warmer than winter in each hemisphere, because the sun's rays hit the Earth at a more direct angle during summer than during winter, and also because days are much longer than nights during the summer.

If the Earth were not tilted, the cold air would stay at the North and South poles and the warm air would stay at the Equator. The tilt and the resulting seasons keep the air masses moving.

In the United States, which is in the Northern Hemisphere, the weather in each of the four seasons is distinctly different. Although conditions may vary from year to year, in general:

WINTER (Dec. 21-March 20) has the coldest temperatures. The precipitation may be rain, freezing rain, sleet or snow. Blizzards, which are blinding snowstorms that last for more than three hours, occur in the winter. During the cold months, you will hear the meteorologist talk about the "wind chill." That is the effect of the wind making the air feel much colder to your skin.

SPRING (March 21-June 20) is when the temperatures warm up from winter. The precipitation may still be snow, but more often it is rain. Most violent storms and flash flooding occur during the springtime.

SUMMER (June 21-Sept. 22) is the hottest time of year. Normally, the high temperatures are between 80 and 90 degrees, although sometimes temperatures may be more than 120 degrees. Afternoon thunderstorms are common in the summertime. Summer storms tend to have a lot of lightning and occasionally hail and strong winds. Severe storms do occur in the summer but are not as frequent as spring. This is because there are not as many strong cold fronts coming through in the summer time.

FALL (Sept. 23-Dec. 20) is when the temperatures begin to cool off. The frequent cold fronts moving across the country produce stormy weather. Hurricanes are more frequent in the Gulf of Mexico and the Atlantic Ocean during fall. Sleet and snow can occur late in the autumn season.

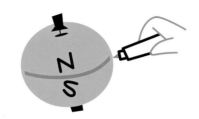

Activity:

Earth Orbits the Sun

Gather:
- Something round to simulate the Earth, like an orange
- Flashlight
- Construction paper
- Magic Marker
- Tape and scissors
- Pushpins

1. Cut a large star out of construction paper. Tape it on a wall. This is your North Star.

2. Place the flashlight in the center of a table.

3. Make four signs that read Winter, Spring, Summer and Fall. Place them on the table in a circle around the flashlight in this order: Winter at the top, nearest the North Star; Spring to the left; Summer at the bottom; and Fall to the right.

4. To make your "globe," draw a circle around the center of the orange and label it "Equator."

Write "N" above the equator to label the Northern Hemisphere and "S" below the equator for the Southern Hemisphere. You can place an extra pushpin or just make a mark to approximate where your hometown is on your globe.

Stick a pushpin in the top of the orange and another in the bottom of the orange to represent the North and South poles.

5. Hold your "globe" so the North Pole tilts towards your North Star, approximately 23.5 degrees. Move it around the flashlight in the way the Earth orbits the sun. It is VERY important to keep your North Pole tilted toward the North Star! You will have to rotate the flashlight with the "globe" so it stays illuminated.

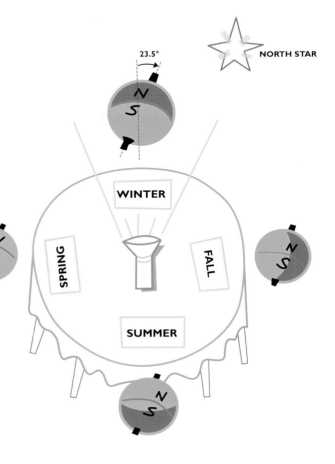

Stop at each season and notice how the flashlight illuminates the Northern Hemisphere more during our summer and less during our winter. Also notice how the illumination is equal north and south of the equator during the fall and spring.

What did you learn?
As the Earth orbits the sun, the sun's angle changes. This makes it warm in the summer and cold in the winter. In the spring, the direct rays of the sun are in transition from the Southern Hemisphere to the Northern Hemisphere. In fall, the sun's direct rays are moving from the Northern Hemisphere to the Southern Hemisphere.

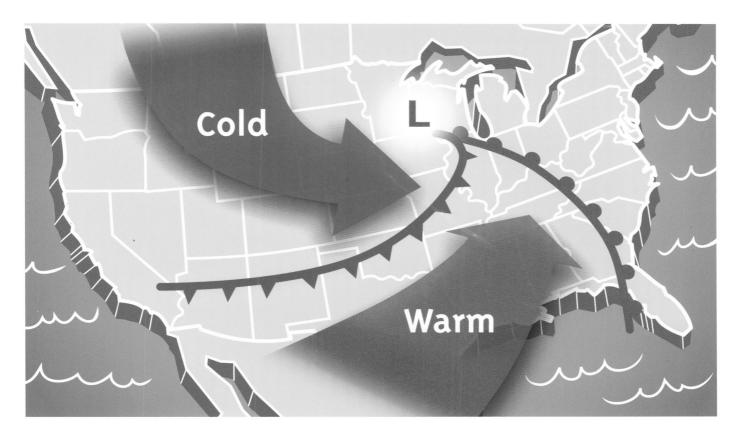

Air Masses

Meteorologists are scientists trained to understand and predict weather. The process of predicting the weather begins with identifying and tracking the different air masses that move across the globe. By monitoring the temperature, dew point, barometric pressure and wind, we can find where the warm-air and cold-air masses are and where they are going. It is also important to track the location and movement of high and low pressure areas.

We draw a cold front along the leading edge of a cold air mass, and we draw a warm front along the leading edge of the warm air mass. The pips and barbs on the front point in the direction the air mass is moving. When these air masses collide, the weather gets very interesting.

One of the weather patterns that produce storms occurs when a moist air mass is forced to rise vertically. This happens in several ways. The most common ways to cause air to lift are:

1. Air is forced to rise when it hits a mountain range. This is called an "orographic lift."

2. An air mass warms. Warm air is lighter than cold air, so sometimes just the heat of the sun can cause air to rise and produce precipitation. This is called "convection."

3. A cold front forces air to rise. As the cold, heavy air collides with the warm, moist air, it acts like a wedge and forces the warm air to rise. This is called "forced lifting" and can produce strong thunderstorms.

Once storms form, meteorologists use tools like Doppler radar to track them. We can tell where the storms are located and what kind of weather they are producing — in the spring, summer and fall, this might be heavy rain, hail, strong winds or a tornado.

Storm-tracking computer software, including Doppler radar, allows a meteorologist to detect rotation in a storm. That can then allow us to predict the chance of a tornado before it touches down.

20,000 ft.

20,000 ft.

High clouds (Cirrus)
These clouds form above 20,000 feet and are usually made of ice crystals.

Vertical Clouds (Cumulus)
These clouds grow upward. They tend to have a flat base and a rounded top. These are the clouds that can grow into thunderstorms within a few hours.

Cloud Types
Basic Categories

Nimbus
If clouds at any level are producing precipitation, "nimbus" is added. For example, a low cloud that is producing a steady rain is called a "nimbostratus." A cumulus cloud that is producing a thunderstorm is called a "cumulonimbus."

15,000 ft.

15,000 ft.

10,000 ft.

10,000 ft.

Mid-level clouds (Alto)
These clouds form between 6,500 and 23,000 feet.

5,000 ft.

5,000 ft.

Low clouds (Stratus)
Stratus means "to cover the sky." Fog is a low stratus cloud.

0 ft.

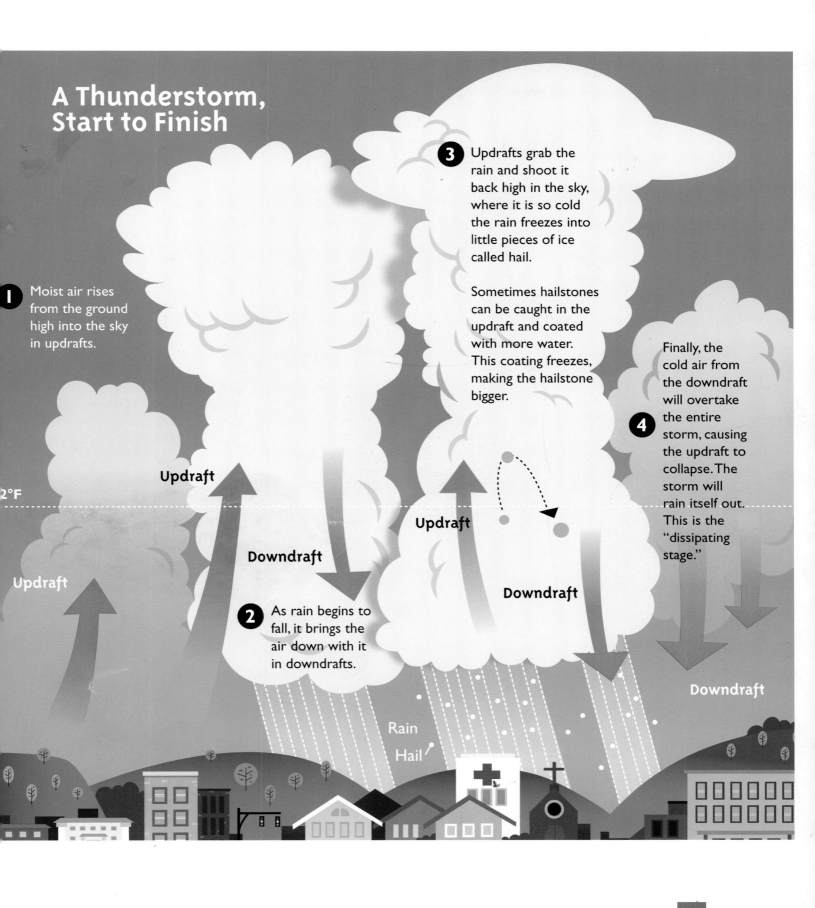

A Thunderstorm, Start to Finish

1 Moist air rises from the ground high into the sky in updrafts.

2 As rain begins to fall, it brings the air down with it in downdrafts.

3 Updrafts grab the rain and shoot it back high in the sky, where it is so cold the rain freezes into little pieces of ice called hail.

Sometimes hailstones can be caught in the updraft and coated with more water. This coating freezes, making the hailstone bigger.

4 Finally, the cold air from the downdraft will overtake the entire storm, causing the updraft to collapse. The storm will rain itself out. This is the "dissipating stage."

Updraft

Downdraft

Updraft

Updraft

Downdraft

Downdraft

32°F

Rain

Hail

Understanding
Severe Thunderstorms

In the middle of the United States, rain occurs often throughout the year, at any time of the day or night. Often it is just rain, with perhaps some thunder, lightning and wind. Sometimes it will rain for several hours, sometimes for a few minutes.

Danger!

A severe storm can have many dangerous effects:
- **Flash flooding** is the most deadly, killing **146** people on average each year.
- **Lightning** is the second deadliest, killing **100** people on average each year.
- **Tornadoes** kill **80** people on average each year.

But sometimes the thunderstorm is much more intense, even becoming severe. A severe storm is defined as having one or more of the following: hail 3/4-inch to 1 inch or more in size, wind gusts of 58 mph or greater, and/or a tornado.

Thunderstorms occur when warm, moist air is forced to rise high into the sky. As the developing storm rises, it is dominated by updrafts. You can see the clouds building and bubbling during this phase.

When the rain begins to fall, it drags the air down with it. This is called a downdraft. When a storm has both downdrafts and updrafts, it is a pretty strong storm.

The updrafts can grab some of the rain and blow it back high in the sky, where it is so cold the rain freezes into little pieces of ice. This is called hail.

When the hail falls back toward Earth, it gets coated with more water. Sometimes the hailstones get caught again in the updraft and pushed high in the sky, where the coating of water freezes, making the hailsto...

...other in th... ...drafts creates a separation of electrical charges in the cloud. The smaller, positively charged ice crystals rise to the top of the cloud, while the bigger, negatively charged ice crystals drop to the lower part of the storm.

The negatively charged bottom of the storm sends an invisible charge toward the ground. When it gets close to the ground, it is attracted by all the positively charged objects on the ground, and a channel is developed. The electrical transfer along the channel is lightning. (More about lightning ahead.)

When the storm is just about over, there will be no more updrafts, only downdrafts as the storm just rains itself out. This is called the dissipating stage.

A Supercell Thunderstorm

A supercell is the strongest thunderstorm and the most likely to produce tornadoes. Here are some things to look for:

Green sky. This occurs because of the way sunlight is refracted through water and hail in a storm. A common belief is that a green sky means a storm will produce a tornado. This is not always the case; many storms produce hail but do not produce tornadoes. But a green sky does indicate a very strong storm.

Wall cloud. This is a rotating lowering in the cloud base. If a tornado forms, it will descend from the wall cloud.

Shelf cloud. As cold air rushes out of the front of the severe thunderstorm, a long, horizontal lowering will be

Anvil

This is the flat, spreading top of a cumulonimbus cloud.

Overshooting top

This domelike protrusion over an anvil indicates a strong updraft.

Mammatus clouds

These rare clouds look like giant boiling bubbles under the anvil of a severe thunderstorm. They indicate very unstable air.

The updraft

It will appear as a cauliflower-looking vertical column. If the updraft is very strong it may have an overshooting top.

The downdraft

This will be where you see the rain and/or hail shaft.

Wall cloud

Shelf cloud

13

Lightning

A storm doesn't have to produce a tornado to be deadly. Lightning kills more people each year than tornadoes. On average, 1,000 people are injured by lightning each year, and 100 are killed by lightning.

The minute you hear thunder, you are at risk of being struck by lightning. It does not have to be raining for lightning to strike you. Lightning can strike up to 10 miles ahead, to the side of or behind a thunderstorm.

Remember, a sudden, surprising shock is called a "bolt from the blue": The sky can be clear overhead, but people have been struck by lightning shooting out from a distant thunderstorm.

Fascinating Facts

- Lightning is about 50,000 degrees Fahrenheit. That is six times hotter than the surface of the sun! The intense heat causes the air to expand rapidly and to vibrate quickly. The sound of this vibration is thunder. The rumbling thunder you hear when a storm is in the distance is caused by the sound bouncing off hilltops and buildings.

- A lightning bolt is only about as wide as a quarter but can be 2 to 5 miles long when traveling from cloud to ground and more than 20 miles long when traveling from cloud to cloud.

Lightning Safety

In Your Home

Your home is usually the safest place to be during an electrical storm. However, it is not perfect. Lightning can travel along copper wires and pipes into your home.

The safest thing to do is to stay at least 3 feet away from all appliances, corded telephones, sinks, bathtubs and toilets. Do not play video games that are attached to your TV by wires. While corded telephones can be dangerous, cell phones and wireless telephones are OK, as long as they are away from the base charging station.

Remain in your home for at least 30 minutes after the last time you hear thunder. Remember, lightning can strike backwards from a thunderstorm. Just because the storm has passed doesn't mean the risk of lightning strikes is over.

In Your Car

It is not the rubber tires that make your car a safe shelter from lightning. Rather, it is the metal cage of the car body that helps redirect the lightning around the outside of the car. Tires sometimes melt from the intense heat of the lightning, but they are not what keep you safe.

While seeking shelter from lightning in your car, be sure to keep your hands away from the windows, steering wheel and keys. You want to avoid contact with anything metal.

Outside

If you are caught outside when a thunderstorm approaches, the safest thing to do is run back to your car or into a sturdy building that has four sides and a roof. Seeking shelter under the awning of a concession stand at a softball game might keep you dry in the rain, but it will do nothing to protect you from lightning.

If there is no place to go, you may have several options that are better than just standing tall in the middle of a field.

1. If the field has tall trees on one side and a cluster of short bushes on the other, crouch as low as you can under the bushes.

2. If the field only has tall trees, move far enough away from the trees so that if they fall, they won't hit you.

• Crouch down, getting as low to the ground as possible without lying down. You want the least amount of your body touching the ground as possible.

• Place your head low and cover your ears to protect them from the acoustical shock of thunder.

3. Move away from other people. Do not gather in groups. Lightning can strike one person and jump to everyone else. Entire herds of cattle have been killed like this.

• Lightning can strike the same place twice. The Empire State Building in New York is struck by lightning more than 25 times a year!

• The odds of being struck by lightning in your lifetime are 1 in 3,000.

• "Heat lightning" is lightning from a storm that is too far away for you to hear the thunder. Sometimes you can see "heat lightning" from 100 miles away. You can hear thunder only when it is 20 to 30 miles away. You can see farther than you can hear.

• Rubber shoes and rubber tires do not protect you from lightning. Lightning that is traveling over 200,000 mph and is hotter than the surface of the sun is not going to suddenly see your tennis shoes, stop, and move in another direction!

Lightning Experiments

Make Lightning

What you'll need
- Aluminum pie pan
- Small piece of wool fabric
- Styrofoam plate
- Pencil with a new eraser
- Thumbtack

What to do
1. Push the thumbtack through the center of the aluminum pie pan from the bottom
2. Push the eraser end of the pencil into the thumbtack.
3. Put the Styrofoam plate upside-down on a table. Quickly, rub the underneath of the plate with the wool for a couple of minutes.
4. Pick up the aluminum pie pan using the pencil as a handle and place it on top of the upside-down Styrofoam plate that you were just rubbing with the wool.
5. Touch the aluminum pie pan with your finger. You should feel a shock. If you don't feel anything, try rubbing the Styrofoam plate again.
6. Once you feel the shock, try turning the lights before you touch the pan again. Check out what you see. You should see a spark!

What did you learn?
Why does this happen? It's all about static electricity. Lightning happens when the negative charges, which are called electrons, in the bottom of the cloud or in this experiment your finger are attracted to the positive charges, which are called protons, in the ground or in this experiment the aluminum pie pan. The resulting spark is like a mini lightning bolt.

Sticking a Balloon to a Wall

What you'll need
- Balloon
- A piece of wool, nylon or fur
- Wall

What to do
1. Blow up the balloon and tie it.
2. Rub the balloon quickly with your piece of wool, nylon or fur.
3. Put the balloon against the wall and let go.
4. Watch what happens. It should stick to the wall.

What did you learn?
Why does this happen? When you rub the balloon, you're covering it with little negative charges. The negative charges are attracted to the positive charges that are in the wall. That's why the balloon 'sticks' to the wall.

Time to Talk

After a severe thunderstorm has passed, parents and children should sit down and talk together about what happened and how they felt. They might ask such questions as:

What does thunder sound like to you?

_____

_____

_____

What is thunder really?

_____

_____

_____

_____

Can thunder by itself hurt you?

_____

_____

_____

How can you stay safe from lightning?

_____

_____

_____

_____

What did you learn from our lightning experiments?

_____

_____

_____

_____

What are some good things about lightning?

_____

_____

_____

How would you rank your fear on a scale from 1-10?
1 = I screamed and cried and was paralyzed with fear.
5 = I kept my head under the blanket.
10 = I monitored the storm, stayed safe and was very brave.

Experiments

Make Thunder

What you need:
• A brown paper lunch bag

What to do
1. Fill the brown paper lunch bag by blowing into it.
2. Twist the open end closed.
3. Quickly hit the bag with your free hand.

What did you learn?
Hitting the bag causes the air inside the bag to compress so quickly that the pressure breaks the bag. The air rushes out and pushes the surrounding air away from the bag. The air continues to move forward in a wave. When the moving air reaches your ear, you hear a sound.

Thunder is produced in a similar way. As lightning strikes, energy is given off that heats the air through which it passes. This heated air quickly expands, producing energetic waves of air, resulting in the sound called thunder.

Count Hailstone Rings

1. When it is safe to do so, ask an adult collect a hailstone and bring it inside.
2. Quickly cut the hailstone in half before it melts.
3. Count the rings.

What did you learn?
This will tell you how many times the hailstone was blown back up to the top of the thunderstorm in the updrafts before it became so heavy it fell to the ground.

Fascinating Fact:

The biggest hailstone ever measured fell in Aurora, Neb., on June 22, 2003. It was almost as big as a soccer ball! It measured 7" in diameter and had a circumference of 18.75."

Understanding the Fear

For Parents

Children are not born afraid. They learn fear from watching people around them. As a parent, you are the child's greatest influence. If you are calm, organized and reassuring, your child will be too!

If you are terrified of severe weather and are unable to model calmness for your child, please consider seeking professional help. You may have had a traumatic severe weather experience that a therapist could help you work through.

Also, if your child has a panic or behavioral disorder, you may need the assistance of a therapist or doctor to work through those issues.

Tools you can use to help your child:

1. If children are terrified by the sounds of thunder and lightning, heavy rain and strong winds, have them listen to a CD or tape of a thunderstorm.

As they do so, have them talk about how those sounds make them feel. Give them new phrases to say aloud while they listen to the tape. Some examples:

• "I know the weather is noisy outside. I am not going to let the sound bother me."

• "Wow! That was loud. I'm really brave tonight."

• "Thunderstorms are crazy but they are also good for the Earth! They bring rain for our flowers, they help clean the air, and the lightning actually gives nutrients to the soil!"

• "It makes me feel good to be so brave during a storm."

Experts say that getting children to make positive statements about a fear can help turn that fear around, especially when Mom and Dad say them, too!

2. Help your child learn what causes severe storms. By understanding how the weather works, your child will learn to be in awe of nature's power.

3. Have your children do experiments that can teach them more about the weather.

4. If you live near a TV station, contact the meteorologist to see if tours of the weather center are given. Sometimes showing a child how meteorologists track storms can reassure her.

5. During a storm, give your child activities to help keep him calm.

6. Always encourage your children to talk about their fears, free from criticism. Don't say, "There's nothing to be afraid of." Instead say, "I know the sound of thunder scares you. Sometimes it scares me, too! But let's work together on becoming brave during the storm."

Don't say, "Your sister's not afraid. You should be like your sister!" Instead say, "Your sister's not afraid. Maybe she can play a game with you during the next storm or talk to you about how she is feeling."

7. When a child has successfully endured a storm with courage and calmness, reward him with praise and encourage him to tell you how it makes him feel to have done such a good job. A psychiatrist once told me that you do not want a child to want you to feel proud of him. You want the child to feel proud of himself.

Example: "Wow, you were very brave during that storm. How does that make you feel?" or, "You were trying very hard to be brave during that storm. Did the lightning still scare you? Do you think you can be even braver next time?"

• Before we learn about tornadoes, have your child tell you how he feels today about tornadoes. Getting a base line on his fear can help him manage it.

Have your child:

1. Draw a picture of a tornado.

2. Write about a past tornado experience, or what he thinks it would be like to be in a tornado.

Understanding Tornadoes

Tornadoes deserve our respect. However, the more you understand about how tornadoes form, how they move and how you can stay safe, the less frightened you will be of them.

Scientists are working to learn the different ways tornadoes form. One simple idea is the "rotating column" theory. When air blows across the land, the friction caused by its movement slows it down. The wind just above the surface blows faster. That can cause a column of air to start to rotate.

When a mature storm moves over one of these horizontally rotating columns of air, the column can get picked up in the updraft, causing it to turn vertically. When the tube is stretched vertically and tightened, it makes a tornado.

Not all tornadoes form in supercell thunderstorms. Sometimes tornadoes can spin up quickly in a fast-moving line of severe thunderstorms called a squall line. It is important to remember that severe thunderstorms can produce a tornado with no warning.

Watches & Warnings

Watches and warnings are issued by different government agencies.

If the weather conditions are right for severe storms to form, the Storm Prediction Center (SPC) will issue a **Severe Thunderstorm Watch**. This means you should continue with your daily routine but keep an eye on the weather and monitor your local radio or TV stations for more information.

If a severe thunderstorm watch has been issued, it is best to stay close to a place where you can seek shelter if you need to.

Once a severe storm has been detected, the local National Weather Service (NWS) will issue a **Severe Thunderstorm Warning**. This means that a storm capable of producing a tornado, large hail and/or winds of 58 mph or stronger is occurring or is likely to occur soon. A meteorologist can now tell where the storm is, what it is doing, where it is going and what time it will get there.

If the conditions are right for storms that may produce tornadoes, the SPC will issue a **Tornado Watch** for a specified area and length of time.

The meteorologists at the National Weather Service and at your local TV stations will be monitoring the weather for any signs that it may produce a tornado. They have high-tech tools such as Doppler radar that help them look inside a storm to see if the winds have started rotating.

Once strong rotation in a storm or a tornado has been spotted, either by Doppler radar or by a trained storm spotter, the NWS will issue a **Tornado Warning** for your county.

In many communities, local emergency personnel in communication with the NWS will sound a siren when a tornado warning is issued so people know to seek shelter immediately.

Remember: Tornado sirens were meant to alert people outside that danger was near. Not all communities have sirens, not all sirens can be heard inside and some storms can produce a tornado too quickly for sirens to be turned on in time. It is best to have an NOAA radio as your primary alert and consider outside sirens a backup.

Tornado Formation

A column of air rotates horizontally as it encounters friction with the earth. A storm's updraft lifts the rotating column of air vertically.

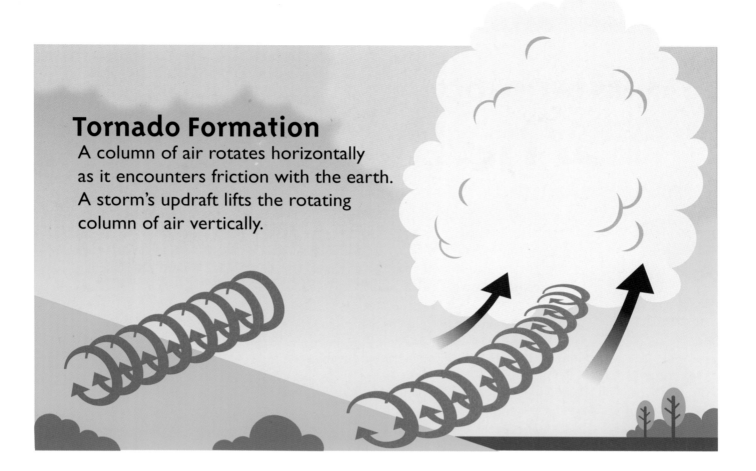

When the column is stretched tight, a tornado forms.

Tornado Experiments

Tornado Column

What you need
- A pencil

What to do
1. Open your hand flat and put a pencil on your palm.
2. Put your other hand on the pencil and roll it on your palm. See how it rotates?
3. Keep rotating the pencil and turn your hands so your thumbs are pointing up.

Now you can see how the column of air went from being horizontal to vertical ... just like a tornado.

Tornado in a Jar

What you need
- Clear liquid soap
- Food coloring and glitter
- Vinegar
- Water
- Clear glass jar with a tight-fitting lid

What you do
1. Fill the jar about three-quarters full of water.
2. Put 1 teaspoon of liquid soap and 1 teaspoon of vinegar into the jar.
3. Add a few drops of food coloring and ? tablespoon of glitter to the jar.
4. Tighten the lid and shake the jar to mix up the ingredients.
5. Holding the top of the jar, twirl the jar in a circular motion. The liquid will form a small tornado.

You can now see how the vortex picks up the glitter as if it were debris from a storm.

Fascinating Facts

Tornadoes can occur any time of day, in any time of the year and in any state across our country. However, tornadoes are more likely at certain places and times.

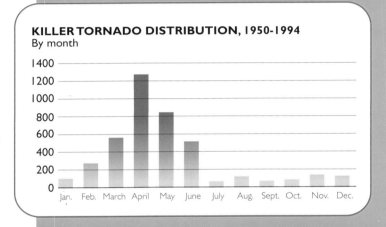

KILLER TORNADO DISTRIBUTION, 1950-1994
By month

- Most tornadoes occur between 2 and 8 p.m.
- Most tornadoes occur in the months of March, April, May and June. However, notice that tornadoes have occurred in every month of the year.

The top 10 states with the most tornadoes are:
1. Texas
2. Oklahoma
3. Kansas
4. Florida
5. Nebraska
6. Iowa
7. Missouri
8. South Dakota
9. Illinois
10. Colorado

In an atlas of the United States, look up these states and see how close together many of them are. That's why the central part of the United States is often called "Tornado Alley."

Keeping Safe During a Tornado

Home

If you have a basement, it is the safest place to be during a tornado.

But it is not enough to just be sitting in your basement. Imagine the worse-case scenario: The roof above you may get blown away. If that happens, you will be sitting in an open pit with debris flying all around you.

So when you are in your basement and the tornado is near, try to put as many walls between you and the outside as possible. Consider taking shelter in a basement bathroom or closet or under the stairs. If those places are not good options, try getting under a sturdy worktable or pool table.

You have to protect your head and neck from flying debris. Have everyone put on bike helmets or football helmets. (I know it sounds and looks funny, but it can honestly save your noggin!)

If you have time before the storm hits, make sure everyone has on sneakers or other sturdy shoes. You don't want to have to walk out of the basement across broken glass with bare feet.

There is no conclusive evidence that one corner is safer than another in your basement, based on the direction storms usually

move. Remember: Tornado winds are rotating, swirling — the debris will be flying in circles. It is just imperative that you protect your head from that flying debris.

Home with no basement

My first advice is to make sure a friend or neighbor has a basement that you can go to in the event of a tornado.

If you don't have time to leave the house, try to get as many walls as possible between you and the outside. Pick a closet, bathroom or hallway without windows, in the center of the house, that you can huddle in until the storm passes.

Remember, you must protect your head and feet. Wear a bicycle helmet or football helmet if you have one. Wrap yourself in blankets and pillows. Some people have been able to survive by lying in their bathtubs with something over them to protect them from flying debris. If you have time, make sure you have your sneakers on.

Manufactured home

Some home manufacturers claim their homes are built to withstand certain wind strengths if the homes are tied down correctly. If you feel your home is sturdy enough, follow the guidelines under "Home with no basement."

However, more often than not, you are going to be much safer if you leave the manufactured home and go to a community storm shelter or a nearby business. Some experts believe you are actually safer seeking shelter outside in a ditch than remaining in a manufactured home during a tornado.

Apartments or hotels

If you are not in a basement apartment, it is important to ask the property manager what the tornado safety plan is. If there is no sturdy building for you to seek shelter in, make arrangements with a nearby friend or neighbor who lives in a house so that you can go there during a tornado watch or warning.

If you are staying at a hotel and severe storms are in the forecast, ask the hotel manager what the plan is. I assure you, most hotels have one. Ask who will be monitoring the weather alerts and how the guests will be contacted to let them know it is time to seek shelter.

Malls and movie theaters

Most large shopping malls and theaters have a tornado shelter and a plan in place to protect their customers. Next time you are at your favorite mall, ask the mall manager or security personnel to tell you about their tornado plan. When in a large building, you must find small spaces such as bathrooms to stay safe.

Schools and churches

You want to avoid big rooms with large, free-span roofs such as gymnasiums, cafeterias and sanctuaries. Always think about getting as many walls as possible between you and the outside and try to get as far underground as possible. If a basement is not available, seek out an interior hall, room or closet.

Automobiles

Experts believe you are safer in a ditch than in your car during a tornado. If you are caught in your car during a tornado and the tornado doesn't appear to be moving in any direction except getting bigger, chances are that it is moving directly toward you.

Since you do not know how fast it is moving or whether you'll have time to outrun it, abandon the vehicle. Find a ditch, culvert, drainage tunnel or a depression in the ground. Get down as low as possible. Cover your head with your arms.

For parents with babies in infant seats, I recommend you leave the child in the infant seat, remove the seat from the car and place it on the ground under your body. Be careful not to suffocate the child.

It is highly advised that you not try to outrun a tornado for many reasons:

• The rain and hail may get so heavy you can't see.

• The road may be blocked by fallen power lines or trees or become impassable due to high water or mud.

• You may turn down a road you are not familiar with and end up at a dead end with no escape route.

Overpasses

Ever since footage of a film crew seeking shelter under an overpass in Kansas was aired, people have had the horrible belief that climbing up to get under the steel or concrete beams of an overpass is a smart thing to do during a tornado. BAD IDEA!!!

Here's why:

• Winds increase with elevation in a tornado. The winds are stronger above the ground because they don't have the friction of the earth to slow them down. You always want to get as low as possible.

Don't climb UP anything to seek shelter from a tornado.

• Winds may accelerate under an overpass because they are being funneled.

• Debris collects under an overpass, therefore your chances of being hurt by flying debris increases.

• The steel/concrete bridge over your head will not be protected from the swirling winds of a tornado that will come at you from all sides.

Parks or lakes

The No. 1 safety rule during severe-weather season is to know the forecast before heading out for long adventures away from a sturdy shelter.

Usually, meteorologists know one to three days in advance if severe weather is a possibility. If you chose to head out on a boat, go golfing or go for a drive out into the country and you know there is a chance for bad weather, take an NOAA weather radio with you (these are available at electronics stores and discount department stores). This will allow you to monitor the weather, plus it will alert you if a warning has been issued for your area.

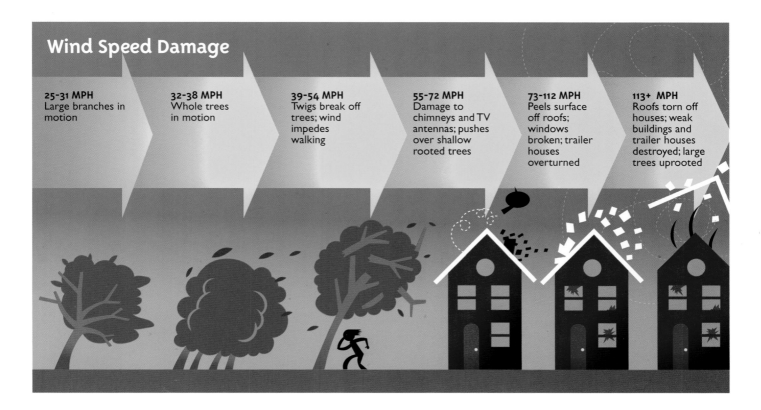

Wind Speed Damage

25-31 MPH Large branches in motion

32-38 MPH Whole trees in motion

39-54 MPH Twigs break off trees; wind impedes walking

55-72 MPH Damage to chimneys and TV antennas; pushes over shallow rooted trees

73-112 MPH Peels surface off roofs; windows broken; trailer houses overturned

113+ MPH Roofs torn off houses; weak buildings and trailer houses destroyed; large trees uprooted

Making a
Plan

Discuss with the whole family what to do in the event of a tornado.
- Where will you go in your home?
- Decide on a meeting place if you should get separated during the storm.
- Do the children know what to do if the parent is unable to make it home before a storm? Designate a neighbor or relative who can be with the children if possible.
- Before severe-weather season begins, pack a Storm Survival Kit.

Storm Survival Kit

Place in sturdy box or backpack:
- First-aid kit
- Flashlight
- Extra batteries
- Extra shoes
- Change of clothes
- Baby items (if needed)
- Bottled water
- List of phone numbers

Activities...

...During the Storm Watch

1. Finish packing your survival kit. To make it fun, pack the kit as if you were planning a picnic. When the time comes to go to your safe place, make it fun: "We're going on a basement picnic!"

In most cases, you do not need to go to your storm shelter until a storm warning has been issued. But it is always best to be prepared. (If it is going to be a stormy night, consider "camping out" in the basement. Perhaps pitch a tent and have everyone sleep in a sleeping bag.) Here is a list of items to place in your shelter while you're under a storm watch:

- Blankets and pillows
- Medicines
- Extra food
- Bike helmets
- Baby car seat
- Favorite stuffed animals.

Keep these items with you until it is time to seek shelter or a storm warning has been issued:

- NOAA weather radio
- Laminated county maps
- Cell phone with extra pre-charged batteries
- Extra cash and a credit card (keep in mind, ATM machines may go down during a bad storm)

2. Gather the family pets. If they have kennels, put them in their kennels in the basement. Try to gather the pets early. Do not risk your safety looking for the pets during the storm.

3. Before the power goes off, play flashlight games. This will help make the power loss less dramatic and also help you check that your flashlights are working.

4. Have older children plot the storm on a map. (Print out your city, county and street maps from the Internet and have them laminated at a copying store.) As you listen to the weather reports, have your children put an X where the storm is being spotted.

The children can check the map to see whether the storm is heading toward you or not. If you have family in the area, have their street labeled as well so you can see how they are doing.

5. Have older children review A Supercell Thunderstorm on Page 13. The progression of most severe thunderstorms is: Approach of the anvil, light rain, moderate rain, green sky, heavy rain and hail. If the supercell storm produces a tornado, it usually occurs after the hail.

If the part of the storm producing the tornado passes to the north or south, you may encounter large hail and very strong winds that can break glass, peel off roofing material and snap small trees. If you are in your safe place, these winds rarely cause bodily harm.

...During the Storm Warning

1. Have special games for these "basement picnics." Play board games or charades, draw pictures or write about your feelings, sing songs and tell stories.

Children can feed off their parents' positive energy. The storm is going to do what it will do, regardless of anyone's stress level. So why not stay calm, encouraging and lighthearted? The lesson children learn will stay with them for a lifetime.

2. Continue tracking the storm on your maps.

3. How close is the storm? Is it moving toward you or away?

Count the seconds between when you see lighting and hear the thunder. Divide that number by 5. This gives you the number of miles distant the storm is.

For example, if you can count to 15 before you hear the thunder, 15 divided by 5 = 3. The storm is 3 miles away. If the number is getting smaller, the storm is approaching. If the number is getting larger, the storm is moving away.

If A Tornado Strikes Your Home

1. When a tornado strike is imminent, protect everyone from flying debris. Get under a sturdy bench or pool table or under the stairs. If you have a bike helmet, put it on; otherwise, cover your head with your arms.

Place babies in car seats and buckle the straps. Use your body, pillows and blankets to protect your children. Be very careful not to cause suffocation.

2. An actual tornado strike usually lasts only a few minutes. Be prepared for a rapid pressure change. Your ears may pop. Expect very loud noises, from the roar of the tornado to the sound of glass breaking, boards splintering and furniture moving. Sometimes the tornado will lift the roof off and slam it back down. If your windows break or walls collapse, you may get pelted with rain and hail.

3. Once the winds have stopped, gather everyone together and assess any injuries. Call 911 if possible. As you climb out of your basement or shelter, be aware of broken glass, floors that may collapse, fallen power lines and items that may fall from above.

Try to keep as much of your storm safety kit with you as possible.

4. Help other injured or trapped neighbors if possible. Check on elderly neighbors who may need assistance.

5. Do not re-enter your home if it has sustained bad damage.

6. Continue to monitor the weather. More storms may be on the way.

After the storm

As soon as possible after a severe storm, discuss the event with the children. If the children are old enough, have them write a story about their experience. Encourage them to write about how they handled their fear and what activities helped the most.

If the children are too young to write out their feelings, have them draw a picture or just talk to you about the experience. Conquering fear is a process supported by positive steps. Take it one storm at a time.

Time to Talk

So we just had a big storm. Tell me about it.

Before you took shelter, what did the sky look like?

_____

_____

_____

What were your feelings as the storm approached?

_____

_____

_____

What did you do to stay calm?

_____

_____

_____

_____

(continued)

What did it sound like as the storm approached?

_____

_____

_____

_____

What happened when the storm hit?

_____

_____

_____

_____

What did you do after the storm?

_____

_____

_____

_____

Rate your bravery during a severe storm experience on a scale from 1-10.
1 = I was paralyzed with fear.
5 = I hid under my bed.
10 = I monitored the storm, stayed safe and was very brave.

Let's Review

Months before storm season

Make a family plan. Prepare your storm survival kit. Start conquering the fear of noisy storms by having your child listen to a storm on a CD. Encourage your children to talk about their fears. Discuss ways to overcome their fears.

During the storm warning

Assign someone to monitor the storm on NOAA weather radio and/or your local TV station. Gather last-minute storm-survival items and head to your safe place. Track the storm. Play special games, read books, sing songs, look at photo albums, etc., to distract children.

When the storm hits

Protect your body from flying debris. Keep as calm as possible. Anyone who has survived a tornado will tell you the fury is horrible, but the wind and the noise will stop. Calm will be restored.

After the storm

When safety and calm have been secured, gather the family together. Call 911. Move away from danger. Help others if you can. When safety and calmness have been secured, talk about the experience.

Glossary

Barometric Pressure: The weight of the atmosphere.

Doppler: Radar that can measure movement of the air toward or away from a radar tower.

Downdraft: A small-scale column of air that rapidly sinks toward the ground, usually accompanied by precipitation, as in a rain shower or thunderstorm. A downburst is the result of a strong downdraft.

Hail: Showery precipitation in the form of irregular pellets or balls of ice more than 5mm in diameter, falling from a cumulonimbus cloud.

Heat Lighting: Lightning that occurs at a distance such that thunder is no longer audible.

Humidity: Generally, a measure of the water-vapor content of the air.

Lightning: A visible electrical discharge produced by a thunderstorm. It may occur within or between clouds, between a cloud and air, between a cloud and the ground or between the ground and a cloud.

Meteorologist: A person who studies the atmosphere, weather and climate. The different areas within the field of meteorology include research meteorologist, radar meteorologist, TV meteorologist, climatologist, or operational meteorologist.

National Weather Service (NWS): An agency of the federal government within the National Oceanic and Atmospheric Administration of the Department of Commerce. It is responsible for providing observations, forecasts and warnings of meteorological and hydrological events in the interest of national safety and economy.

Web Resources

www.weatherwizkids.com/
This is a great site written for children by a TV meteorologist. It includes many weather experiments.

eo.ucar.edu/webweather/
This Web site for children is by the Center for Atmospheric Research.

www.spc.noaa.gov
This is where meteorologists go to forecast severe weather.

www.weather.gov
The National Weather Service site is a great place to get your forecast.

www.nssl.noaa.gov/edu/safety/
The National Severe Storms Laboratory has more information on severe weather safety.

Precipitation: Falling products of condensation in the atmosphere, such as rain, snow or hail; also, the amount of rain, snow, hail etc. that has fallen at a given place within a given period, usually expressed in inches of water.

Severe Thunderstorm: A thunderstorm that produces a tornado, winds of at least 58 mph and/or hail at least 3/4 inch in diameter.

Supercell: A thunderstorm consisting of one rotating updraft that may exist for several hours. It generates the vast majority of long-lived strong and violent tornadoes, as well as downburst damage and large hail.

Thunder: The sound caused by rapidly expanding gases in a lightning discharge.

Thunderstorm: A local storm produced by a cumulonimbus cloud and accompanied by lightning and thunder.

Tornado: A violently rotating column of air, usually descending from a cumulonimbus, whose circulation reaches the ground. It nearly always starts as a funnel cloud and may be accompanied by a loud roaring noise. On a local scale, it is the most destructive of all atmospheric phenomena.

Updraft: A small-scale current of rising air. If the air is sufficiently moist, the moisture condenses to become a cumulus cloud or an individual tower of a towering cumulus

Weather: The state of the atmosphere with respect to wind, temperature, cloudiness, moisture, barometric pressure etc. "Weather" refers to these conditions at a given point in time (for example, today's high temperature), whereas "climate" refers to the average weather conditions for an area over a long period of time (such as the average high temperature for today's date).

Weather Satellite: Manufactured satellites orbiting the Earth that gather information about upper air temperature, humidity, temperature of the clouds, movement of the clouds, water vapor and solar activity. Satellites also relay data from weather instruments around the world. In most TV weather reports, "the satellite" refers to a map that shows the clouds in motion.

A Tribute

The weather can certainly be scary here in the United States. But imagine what it is like for children who live in smaller, less wealthy countries such as Haiti. One heavy rainstorm can wash away their homes and their families. Many of these children are among the 143 million orphans around the world.

C3 Missions International Inc., founded by my friends Beth and Mike Fox, reaches out to these children. The Foxes bring people together to provide culturally relevant homes, not institutional orphanages, in underprivileged communities around the world. What started as a dream to create one such home in Thailand has blossomed into numerous homes in Haiti, Thailand, Cambodia, Uganda and several other African countries. C3's growth is limited only by the number of people willing to say "Yes" to hope.

Please go to **www.c3missions.org** to learn more about this incredible organization. You have already begun to help by purchasing this book, because a portion of the proceeds will go to C3! And 100 percent of donations to C3 go directly to meet children's needs.

Thank you.
Katie Horner